FATHERS

The Heart of the Father — The Cry of the Sons

Deborah Dekker

A father to the fatherless, a defender of widows is God in His holy habitation. God sets the solitary in families; He brings out those who are bound into prosperity.

Psalm 68:5–6

From the prophet even to the priest everyone deals falsely.

For they have healed the hurt of the daughter of My people slightly, saying "Peace, peace!" when there is no peace. ...

The cry of the daughter of My people from a far country:

> *Is not the Lord in Zion?*
> *Is not her King in her? ...*
> *Is there no balm in Gilead?*
> *Is there no physician there?*

Why then is there no recovery for the health of the daughter of My people?

Jeremiah 8: 10–11; 19–22

I have known Deborah for several years and am honoured to call her a dear friend. I hope this will be the first of many books to come from her pen. It is now more than 20 years since the move of God we call the "Father's heart" arrived on the spiritual scene. Now once again we are searching desperately to find our identity as sons and daughters and to find those who are secure enough to father and mother us. Deborah expresses the heart cry of so many in this little book. She is a true daughter of Belgium whose great love for her nation I have found infectious and challenging. Let yourself be challenged again by her words and draw near to the Father's heart for yourself.

Anne Griffith,
prophetic ministry, United Kingdom

This book is challenging, beautiful, disturbing, deep, penetrating, and touches the emotions. I personally was provoked and challenged by its seeming simplicity yet depth. I love the way the Scriptures are blended into it and want to read it again and again. I believe the Holy Spirit has anointed Deborah for this task and what we have here is an anointed book.

Barbara Smith,
prophetic ministry, Scotland

We are so stirred that God has called Deborah to write this book on the right time. This book is a must-read! Deborah shares on a theme that is crucial for the Christian family. She is a woman of prayer and writes out of that place. This book is a whisper of truth to your heart. It leads you to become aware and rise up to the call that God has placed on your life… It is an awakening call for fathers and sons, prodigals and older sons—for churches to be prepared. Let he who has an ear hear, rise up, align with God's plans, and follow Him in His ways…

Luc and Agnès Depreter,
One in Christ Conference, Belgium

This book is so much needed for such a time as this! It is compelling to read a spiritual mother's heart cry for a fathering movement to arise in the Body of Christ. This book has a perfect balance in mastering the art of easy reading and is yet so profound in dissecting the matter by prophetically discerning the times we're living in. It's a pleasure to unpack every few sentences by leaning back and letting the depth of them sink in. It makes you run back to the Father in prayer and bible meditation. Deborah knows how to bring it to a personal level as well as to a macro level, the Church.

Peter Parthoens,
Founder of *Fathering Belgium.org*, Belgium

Fathers : The Heart of the Father — The Cry of the Sons

© Text: Deborah Dekker 2019

Published by Armour Books
P. O. Box 492, Corinda QLD 4075 AUSTRALIA

Cover Image:
© "Harvest Season", copyright Wytze Valkema 2019, www.studiojmarts.nl
Interior Design and Typeset by Book Whispers

ISBN: 978-1-925380-18-7

A catalogue record for this book is available from the National Library of Australia

All rights reserved. No part of this publication may be reproduced, stored in, or introduced into a retrieval system, or transmitted, in any form, or by any means (electronic, mechanical, photocopying, recording or otherwise) without the prior written permission of the publisher.

Unless otherwise indicated, Scripture quotations are taken from the New King James Version. Copyright © 1982 by Thomas Nelson, Inc. Used by permission. All rights reserved.

Scripture quotations marked ESV are taken from the ESV® Bible (The Holy Bible, English Standard Version®), copyright © 2001 by Crossway, a publishing ministry of Good News Publishers. Used by permission. All rights reserved.

Scripture quotations marked NLT are taken from the Holy Bible, New Living Translation, copyright 1996, 2004. Used by permission of Tyndale House Publishers, Inc., Wheaton, Illinois 60189. All rights reserved.

Scripture quotations marked TLB are taken from The Living Bible copyright © 1971 by Tyndale House Foundation. Used by permission of Tyndale House Publishers Inc., Carol Stream, Illinois 60188. All rights reserved.

Table of Contents

Foreword vii

A Word about and from the Writer x

The Cry 2
   1. Fathers 3
   2. Orphans 6

The Challenge 8
   1. The orphan, the widow, the stranger and the poor ... 9
   2. Stepfathers, grandfathers, godfathers 11
   3. Fathers and hirelings 14
   4. Who is the father? 17
   5. Deaf and blind fathers 21
   6. Younger and elder sons 24
   7. Fathers or pharaohs? 26
   8. Sons and daughters coming of age 29
   9. Where are the fathers? 32

The Answer 36
   1. Let the wind blow and the prophet prophesy 37
   2. Let the scribe write 40
   3. Let saviours arise 42
   4. Prodigals coming home 45

Afterword: About the Coming Wind 48

Acknowledgements 51

Foreword

I WROTE THIS BOOK BECAUSE I saw it in a dream. The cover, pale yellow, with the red thread all around, reminding me of the type of cover that a very prestigious publishing house in France has used for decades. Reminding me of the blood of sacrifice also. Then the title appeared, as written by an invisible pen. Surprisingly, it was in English: *Fathers*. An English title for a French-speaking writer; and fathers in the plural. What could that mean?

It took me some time to figure it out. Then, after some months reflecting and praying about this book, this is what I heard, in answer to the question I asked:

What should the book be about?

The book should be about fathers, plural, different kinds of fathers.

First, the Father Who I am; defender of the orphans, defender of the widows and strangers. The One who was ready to give His very life for mankind, to redeem them from their errors.

Then, My leaders, who are supposed to represent Me to the people. Some are good shepherds, some mercenaries. They do not feed the flock but feed on the flock. They are fat whilst my sheep are weak, some ready to die. They don't care, they don't care enough. THEY ARE NOT READY TO GIVE THEIR LIFE FOR THE FLOCK.

This is misrepresenting Me towards My people.

And this thing of tithes and offerings—this insistence on receiving them—this is not from Me, this is not My heart. Was I begging for money during My time on this earth? Surely I was not. I was depending on My Father to provide for My every need. And He did. Faithfully, He provided over and over again. He owns the cattle on many hills. He is the Great Provider, not the one begging for money.

And yes, there are some topics you would prefer not to tackle in your book, but I ask, My daughter, that you would follow Me in obedience. A time of reformation is at hand and I need My prophetic voices and pens to spread the sound and words that will release the shakings. For many shakings are on the way. Once again I will shake the heavens and the earth and uncover the unrighteous foundations that have been laid down by men, even in My Name. I shall clear My Name of any association with those unjust practices; My Name I will make Holy again, separate, distinct from the practices and preferences of other gods. My Name shall be sanctified and glorified once again.

Other fathers need to be named: the robbers, the false prophets, false apostles, false teachers. The ones who exploit and abuse My people. The ones who pretend to speak in My Name, yet I have not sent them. They speak their own words, from their own hearts. I have not sent them, yet they go, they run, they spread their words and sounds, causing confusion in My camp. They spread their own revelation, their own so-called gospel.

A father provides.
A father defends.
A father protects.
A father shares and gives his life.
A father nurtures, as a mother does.

A father calls destiny into being, encourages and develops the talents of his children, both boys and girls. I insist on that aspect, both boys and girls, they are equally called, with plans and purposes assigned to them.

I have My Deborahs, Daniels, Esthers, Samuels, all need to be called and trained, all need to be brought into maturity.

Write!
Tell them that I care! Reconnect the hearts of My children to Mine. Spread the truth and good news once again: I have given My life for them, each one of them! Tell them, again! Write it on the wall, for all to see. Write it on their hearts.

Don't delay!

A word about and from the writer

I AM WRITING THIS FROM a special country. A country which—to a certain extent—is itself an orphan. It was created as a buffer zone in Europe following the defeat of Napoleon at Waterloo.

The British and the Austrians presided at its birth with the Dutch and Germans leaning over the cradle. France ceded a small part of its territory to allow it to come into existence; so too did the Netherlands. The mother tongue of its inhabitants has always been problematic along with its national identity.

Belgium, for this is the country in question, is also the country of the two murdered girls Julie and Melissa,[2] of the 'white marches'—the country of 'the lost children', as the mother of Melissa wrote, 20 years after the disappearance of her daughter.

A country where certain deep wounds are difficult to heal, where healing balm seems to be missing. Where the voices which could cry out to make complaints and demand justice seem to be lacking—or at least fail to make enough noise.

Where the question of the validity of presenting one's case whether before a human or heavenly judgment seat can fail at the crucial moment.

Where the Church, called to defend the widow and the orphan as

---

2   This refers to the "Dutroux case", which shook Belgium in the midst of the 1990s.

well as the mourning parent, often itself seems dumb or paralysed.

I also write from a special point of view.

On the one hand, I had the tremendous privilege of having had a good father, approachable, affectionate, upright, ready to defend me, to raise his voice for me as necessary. On the other hand, I also experienced the great pain at losing this father, suddenly, without warning, leaving me an orphan at the age of 12 with a widowed mother who was completely disorientated.

As my father was originally from the Netherlands, we were Protestants, a confession of faith which, for historical reasons, is very much in the minority in Belgium. Although I shall not develop the historical reasons for this here, let's just say that the Duke of Alba left his stamp on our area.

It is from this triply marginalised position—as a Belgian, as a Protestant and as someone who has lost her father—that I write.

I hope above all that the Wind of the Spirit will inspire my writing and carry it to the ears of those who need to hear this message. And I pray that fathers will arise to encourage the following generations, aware of their role to stand in the gap.

It's not yet too late, but it is certainly time!

Finally, I write precisely at a time where spiritual fathers and mothers have begun to emerge in my country and in my own life, foreshadowing the start of a response to the cry of the orphan heart. Perhaps these father hearts have been there for a long time, or perhaps it has taken all these years to disentangle them from rigid, sclerotic structures in order to get back on the road towards more life-giving family relationships.

May the following words help to enlarge the road back. Back to the Father's heart.

The Cry

1. Fathers

A father to the fatherless, a defender of widows is God in His holy habitation. God sets the solitary in families; He brings out those who are bound into prosperity.

Psalm 68:5–6

Fathers.
We are in need of them.
A fatherless generation is crying out for adoption.
Orphans, all over the world, in and outside the church, are desperately crying out for fathers.
Few are those who respond. Few are those who hear the cry.
Hopes are scattered, bombs are exploding, new hopes are scattered.

An endless and vicious circle of suffering arises and there is almost no one to give sense, show direction or put words to hard-to-understand and heart-breaking situations.

Meanwhile every Sunday crowds gather around preachers who pronounce the law, give motivational speeches and do the stuff they feel they are supposed to do according to the denomination they represent.

General truths are shared which often leave personal needs unattended.

Words are spoken which do not always make personal sense.

Words are offered whilst in fact arms and hearts are needed to embrace and provide a home to hurting children, orphan-spirited crowds. A faceless generation is waiting for fathers to restore identity, name and shape who they are.

Is anyone hearing their cry?

Will anyone respond?

Mothers give birth.

Fathers give life. They impart the gift of life to sons and daughters.

They also call into life what is dormant in them, what has not yet been developed or what has been diminished or repressed by unfavourable circumstances.

Fathers provide, defend, protect.

Fathers call destiny into being; they encourage and develop the talents of their children.

True fathers do not only proclaim the law, they model it; they not only speak but they act upon their own words, they embody what they preach.

For though you might have ten thousands instructors in Christ, you do not have many fathers, says the Bible in 1 Corinthians 4:15.

Instructors pronounce words and send you home to meditate upon them. They're not always available when you have questions.

Instructors give a certain amount of time a day to teach you. They're rarely there outside of this timeframe to provide answers to what life has been throwing at you that same day, outside their classroom.

Instructors are with you, behind a lectern, during the day. They're not eating at your table or comforting you during the night.

Instructors speak to you. They don't expect much response. Fathers share with you. They are interested in hearing what you have to say, what you think, your view upon the subject.

Instructors are in your life for a few months or a few years. They're not there to stay, nor do they expect you to come back after graduation. Fathers are there for a lifetime; their job does not stop after you enter adulthood or receive your first paycheque. It's the role of a lifetime, theirs and yours.

Fathers do not preach at you from a pulpit, once a week at set times. You do not need to make an appointment one month beforehand in order to meet with them. You can call unexpectedly and receive a warm welcome. You can come uninvited and be welcomed with open arms.

Fathers sometimes surprise you with presents—they don't insist on you paying your way. The first hope of a father is to see you prosper, as your soul prospers, not that the family business will prosper through you.

A father is firstly interested in you as an individual and not as a member of a community. He knows and calls you by name; he does not muddle you up with your brothers or sisters.

How many real fathers do we have in our churches today?

Do you know any?

2. Orphans

Pure and undefiled religion before God the Father is this: to visit orphans and widows in their trouble and to keep oneself unspotted from the world.

James 1:27

Orphans.
Orphans of all ages.
Little ones, babies in need of bodily care.
Children looking for protection.
Teenagers in search of guidance.
Adults, young and old, still waiting for comfort, an ear, a hand on their shoulders, someone to say,
"I see you, I hear you, I understand; you're not alone in this."
Even elderly people, even some on their death beds, still waiting for a father's embrace.

Orphans of all kinds, from all nations.
Orphans from Uganda, Rwanda, Burundi, Brazil, Syria—traumatised by war and lack of food, tormented by images and sounds, memories erupting even into their dreams, captives of what was forced upon them.
Orphan-soldiers, victims transformed into tormenters, led into numbing their pain by sowing further destruction all around them. Orphans suddenly deprived of one or both of their parents by

sickness, accident or war, having to face the loss on their own, without meaningful support.

Orphans-with-fathers inhabiting beautiful houses, with gardens, parks and ponies—but feeling all alone as Dad works himself to death, providing wealth to fill the gap in his own emptiness.

Spiritual orphans, seated in churches, incorporated into the system, hearing the father-son rhetoric with a hole in their hearts, unable to identify, to feel warmth with the message, seeing in the preacher another version of the 'infallible' teachers who share their knowledge and cross their path without really showing the Way.

Does anybody care?

Is my life important?

Would someone make time to listen to my story, my hopes, my scattered dreams, my hurts, the obstacles in my way when I try to get up and start again, trying to build out of the ashes?

Am I part of this X-generation, the sacrificed one that no one sees?

Does someone hear me when I cry?

Is anybody there?

The Challenge

1. The orphan, the widow, the stranger and the poor

Cursed is the one who perverts the justice due the stranger, the fatherless and widow.

Deuteronomy 27:19

The Lord watches over the strangers; he relieves the fatherless and widow.

Psalm 146:9

Orphans, widows and strangers. The poor, too.
At the centre of God's care and attention.
Orphans, widows and strangers—often at the periphery of church activities.
If assisted at all, they are not part of the mainstream public, but distinct groups we reach out to by sending money, food or clothes, mostly abroad: orphans in Africa, widows in India, strangers at downtown shelters for the homeless.
The doors of our structures are not yet open to receive them, attend to their needs or incorporate them into our family.

What would a family look like, if it were made up of orphans, widows, strangers and the poor?
Would normal Sunday-morning preaching do?
Would our schedule have to be re-arranged?

Would the singing of hymns be enough?
Wouldn't more of God's presence and love be necessary to attend to these very special people, with their very special needs, hurts and pain?

Orphans—they will need fathers, not leaders over-occupied with the running of programmes, the maintenance of buildings or the preparation of sermons.
Widows (and divorced and singles)—they will require some extra fellowship and support, some practical help also, not hearing that everyone is too busy with the needs of their own family.
Strangers—they will need some space to adapt, to feel at home, overcome trauma for some of them, not to be asked to adapt and conform to our way of doing church, so that we can continue feeling at home.

Would our present structures be adequate when these kinds of people, dear to God's heart, start to queue at our doors? Would we acknowledge and welcome them as members of the family, real brothers and sisters? Would we open our doors and hearts, share our homes and meals with them?

The orphan, the widow, the stranger and the poor: they are often listed in a row, as if they form a community of their own. Loss, isolation, lack, a feeling of marginalisation and difference: these are some of the things they have in common.

Will we leave them there, at the periphery of our assemblies, or will we incorporate them into our family? Will we ourselves agree to be transformed by such an adoption?

2. Stepfathers, grandfathers, godfathers

For though you might have ten thousands instructors in Christ, you do not have many fathers.

1 Corinthians 4:15

My little children, for whom I labour in birth again until Christ is formed in you.

Galatians 4:19

God has no grandchildren, only children.

He has not delegated our care to a third party, nor is He only there for us on weekends or holidays. He cares about our everyday life.

- *Has my son come to a crossroads where it would be important for him to get some extra counsel so that he would not miss out on the next step?*
- *Has my daughter come of age and should marry?*

These are the kind of questions that a father would gladly take into consideration—and not as an obligation. A father cares about these kinds of questions. They matter to him.

He's there on the good days and the bad days; he sees us at our best and our worst.

He honours us when we do our best and corrects us when we are at our worst.

A father disciplines his son when necessary, whilst a grandfather often overlooks the faults, "candycoating" the truth about his son's son's flaws (and daughter's too). Grandparents often have a tendency to indulge their grandchildren.

Also, there's a great difference between God the Father and a Godfather. A father is present in our everyday life. A godfather is only present at the "big events" of our life: baptism, marriage and death—often to play proxy if the actual father has died. In the worst of cases, the godfather figure could be like the one portrayed by Marlon Brando in Scorsese's trilogy: a Corleone more interested in securing his business and position than in protecting your life and securing your future.

A father helps you grow according to your identity and calling.

A godfather could try to turn you into something you're not supposed or called to be and put you in a position you're not supposed to occupy, just to secure an heir for his business or a name for himself.

There are godfathers who have imprinted their image so deeply on their godsons or goddaughters that it is the godfather's image that we see and hear in them, as if an outfit had been passed over to them that they try to fit into. We think here of King Saul handing over his armour to David, making it difficult for the young man to move.

On the other hand, we think of Hannah who, every year, brought a new coat to little Samuel her son, as the child had grown and the mother was careful to provide clothes that would grow with him and not restrict him in any way.

As for stepfathers, they rarely enter your life at your birth. They usually arrive later on, when they enter your family through the remarriage of your mother. Although they can be very efficient channels of love and/or successful in their parenting role to you, you are not flesh of their flesh and they rarely go through birth pains to extricate you from messy chapters in your life.

This being said, here's a question we should probably consider about the leaders in our churches and our relationship to them: grandfathers, stepfathers, godfathers or real fathers—what are they to us?

They are often called "spiritual fathers"—although Jesus said to call no one "father", except His Father in heaven.

What could the reason be?

3. Fathers and hirelings

"I will seek what was lost and bring back what was driven away, bind up the broken and strengthen what was sick."

Ezekiel 34:16

"I am the good shepherd. The good shepherd gives His life for the sheep. But a hireling, he who is not the shepherd, one who does not own the sheep, sees the wolf coming and leaves the sheep and flees; and the wolf catches the sheep and scatters them. The hireling flees because he is a hireling and does not care about the sheep."

John 10:11–13

A father cares about his sons and daughters. So much so that he is often ready to give his life if that would help save theirs.

Fathers stand in the gap for their children. Fathers throw their own body in the battle if necessary. As we see in the story of *The Lion King*, they utter a big roar in the face of the enemy so as to amplify that of their young son, protecting him and backing him up in the fight. Fathers are present when and where it matters, where they are needed to make a difference.

They don't flee when they see trouble come; they don't play it safe if this means exposure for their son or daughter. If there is a battle to turn at the gate, they are there, leading the fight; they are there on the frontline of intercession or spiritual warfare; not hiding in the palace as other warriors take the beating and risk their lives on the frontline.

They fight for the integrity of their heirs.[2] A good father leaves an inheritance to his son's son. He hopes and works to pass something of value on to the next generation. It would be the greatest catastrophe for him to hear that, after his death, his sons would become "*eunuchs in the palace of the king of Babylon.*"[3]

He would not rejoice about having escaped this fate for himself. As a Joshua, a father battles to expand his territory, to transmit a more abundant life, one of fertility not castration, to the next generation. Castration is an ugly perspective: no more chance to reproduce or multiply, the chain of life interrupted, abortion of what could and should have come after him...

If there's one thing a true father would not do, it is this: he would never pass his own sons through the fire; sacrificing them for his own benefit; offering them in exchange for more power, wealth or prominence. A father who would do that would end up like a ravenous wolf—becoming the exact threat he was supposed to protect his son from. Little Simba's Uncle Scar in *The Lion King* offers a picture of such a "parental figure".

Secondly, when it comes to his son or his daughter, a true father does not retreat into passivity. He actively engages in recovering what is lost, repairing what is broken, healing what is hurting in his sons and daughters. He does not take a backseat hoping for the best to happen, for the recovery to take place automatically or for a Samaritan to bring back his lost, wounded child.

The father of the demon-possessed boy in the Bible provides an illustration of a father pursuing healing and deliverance for his

---

[2] See in Amos 3:12: *As the shepherd rescues from the mouth of the lion two legs, or a piece of an ear...*
[3] See Isaiah 39:7

son, his only child. The son's life being in jeopardy, as evil spirits constantly try to push him into water or fire, the father goes to see Jesus' disciples, asking for help.[4] The disciples try to cast the demons out, but without success. Then, they send the man and his demon-possessed son away. No proposal to wait for Jesus, no excess of compassion while sending away father and son with the life-threatening problem unresolved.

Then Jesus returns, and we see him react in a very interesting way to the whole episode. First, He delivers and restores the lunatic boy to health and to his father. In the process He also utters strong words no-one in the crowd probably expected: *"O faithless and perverse generation, how long shall I be with you and bear with you? This kind can only come out by prayer and fasting."*

What could have justified those seemingly harsh words of Jesus ?

Could it be the fact that the father was magically waiting for a miracle from Jesus, without having really searched his own heart about the possible cause for the boy's condition (sin? generational iniquity? idol worship?) Could it be that Jesus was also indirectly addressing his disciples, encouraging them to minister from a father's heart, entering prayer and fasting where needed rather than sending away the boy with an unresolved deadly issue?

And what was the rebuke about? Jesus' words seem to link a lack of effectiveness in ministry with a lack of (sufficient) prayer and fasting.

Jesus does not say: "This deliverance was really a tough one today! I understand that you had to leave it to Me!" He says: "For this kind of problem, more prayer and fasting is required on your part."

Do we pray and fast (enough) in our churches?
Do we set the demon-possessed free?
Do we really want to?

---

[4] See Luke 9:37 or Mark 9:14 for the whole story.

4. Who is the father?

Doubtless You are our Father, though Abraham was ignorant of us and Israel does not acknowledge us. You, O Lord, are our Father, our Redeemer from Everlasting is Your Name.

Isaiah 63:16

Fathers are the head of the family. The head is located on top of the body; you would not expect to find it elsewhere and, if located elsewhere... we have a problem.

Sometimes, in families, fathering is taken over by other members of the family rather than the father: the mother, the son, even the daughter.

If children end up fathering their (younger) brothers or sisters, this has an exhausting effect on them in the long run. If, on top of this, they end up parenting their own fathers or mothers because of some issue or deficiency (alcoholism, drug addiction, profound immaturity or incapacity), the consequences are devastating.

There's a word in psychological language to describe this situation: it is "parental inversion". One of the children ends up in the position of the father, effectively acting as the head of the family, the provider and protector. Of course, this leaves his or her own (inner) child unprotected, un-nurtured and very vulnerable.

"All the animals of field and forest are Mine! The cattle on a thousand hills!"

Psalm 50:10 TLB

If God were hungry, He would not tell us. He does not need our resources, our money. He does not need His children to provide for Him, parent Him, protect Him. He gladly allows us to contribute, joining Him in the harvest field and the building of His Kingdom, but not as His providers. Parental inversion is not something that God practises; more than that, it's something that He forcefully rebukes. It is abusive, contrary to His creation plan and law. And we constantly find Him in the Bible on the line of defence, protecting the weakest.

Genealogies, the succession of generations, is something He keeps an eye on. The identity of the father is an important question for Him. Messing with the generational order He has established is not a small thing.

In His eyes, rebellion is as the sin of witchcraft. And parental inversion is rebellion against His order…

Let's consider Lot: he was a very strange father to his daughters. Offered them as sexual partners in order to protect his male visitors who would otherwise have been molested by the lusting men of his city of Sodom.

"You may do to them as you wish"—terrible words issued by a father about his daughters.[5]

Of course, the immense importance of being hospitable and defending the interests of the guests under his roof provides some explanation to Lot's attitude. Yet the girls must have heard the words and felt like items for sale in a shop.

---

[5] Genesis 19:8

The Bible does not record the names of the two girls—they are only referred to as "Lot's daughters". Maybe because they were presented less as human beings than as objects? Faceless and nameless are the daughters of Lot. They are only referred to by their father's name.

Later on, we meet these two young women again. No longer are they innocent or naïve. *"You may do to them as you wish."* Maybe those words were still resounding in their ears when, in exile in the mountains, without young men to provide heirs for them, they decided to make their father drunk, lie with him and conceive through him? So were Moab and Ben-Ammi born, sons of their grandfather and also father... Sons of their mothers and also sisters...

Not much has been written about the sons of Lot, Moab and Ben-Ammi. However their names are mentioned, names unlike that of their mothers and half-sisters. Later on, they themselves father the Moabites and Ammonites, often referred to in the Bible. Now here comes a point worth noting: the Ammonites were known for the very peculiar god they worshipped. His name was Molech or Moloch, also called Baal-Marduk, a god who fed on child-sacrifice.[6]

"You may do to them as you wish." Those words opened the door to the sacrifice of Lot's daughters. Who then, as a result of incest, conceived sons who would have their sisters as mothers. How much of a blessing can that be? How can this form a firm foundation for identity?

When the place of the father is unclear, perverted or reversed, children end up sacrificed.

Is it such a surprise that this family line would then participate in Baal-worship?

---

[6] More can be read about this in 1 Kings 11:33, 2 Kings 21:6, 2 Kings 16:3 and 2 Kings 17:17. The Israelites were specifically forbidden to give their seed to Moloch (see Leviticus 20:2) or pass their sons or daughters through the fire (see Jeremiah 32:35 or Amos 5:26 for a rebuke about Moloch worship).

Turn away from God the Father to a bloodthirsty "godfather"?[7]

"You may do to them as you wish."

---

[7] For the difference between the God of Israel and Moloch, it is reflected in the etymology of the names: 'Yahweh' alludes to being ('I am that I am'), while 'Baal' ('master') and 'Moloch' ('king') refer to human relations of power and domination. See: Andrew Collier, *On Christian Belief: A Defence of a Cognitive Conception of Religious Belief in a Christian Context*, Routledge Studies in Critical Realism 2003, page 94, for more on this.

5. Deaf and blind fathers

Now the boy Samuel ministered to the Lord before Eli. And the word of the Lord was rare in those days; there was no widespread revelation.

1 Samuel 3:1

Eli was ninety-eight years old and his eyes were so dim that he could not see.

1 Samuel 4:15

And Samuel was afraid to tell Eli the vision.

1 Samuel 3:15

Samuel's story, in the Old Testament, is a very touching one.

The young boy had been born after long years of waiting; his mother Hannah had dedicated him to the service of the Lord. Little Samuel was now serving in the temple, under the guidance of Eli, the priest.

It is a moment in the history of Israel when God seems to have been silent; His words had been few; Eli and his sons held the priesthood and occupied the function. The sons brought in such defilement by their immorality, and Eli by his neglect, that they were quite unable to connect with God and connect the people with Him.

In the midst of this great silence, during the night, Samuel heard his name being called: "*Samuel!*"

The boy got up and presented himself to Eli: "*Here I am, for you have called me!*"

This happened three times. The first two times, the priest addressed these interesting words towards the one he was preparing for the Lord's service: "*I did not call, my son; lie down again.*"

Do you realise what is at stake at this moment, in this exchange, after the word of the Lord had been rare in the land for a long period of time?

In the dialogue where three voices are involved, one of them risks being silenced once again.

Samuel! – the Lord was calling.

Here I am! – Samuel answered. But he was answering Eli, the priest, who was supposed to be the mediator between man and God. Supposed to recognise the Voice.

Lie down again! – Eli, the priest, invited Samuel—the one who had been called—to ignore the word and return to sleep.

This happened twice, before the voice of God called a third time.

How much time elapsed between the three callings recorded in the third chapter of 1 Samuel? The Bible does not say. It could have been a few minutes. It could have been a few days. It could have been a few years.

Twice, little boy Samuel was invited by his spiritual father to ignore the voice and lie down again.

Go to sleep, my son, and tomorrow we'll carry on with priesthood and business as usual. Nothing new under the sun. No new word or sound in the land.

Do you grasp what was at stake here?

Do you marvel at little Samuel's heart and perfect faithfulness to Eli, answering him when he is called?

Do you marvel at his ability to obey Eli, go to sleep twice, and yet manage in this sleep to hear the Voice again?

Do you weep with him at the moment he realises that he had been placed in the position of mediator, hearing from God and having to inform Eli that judgment had come upon his house and that his time of priesthood was now coming to an end?

Do you see little Samuel weep as his ear and heart distance him from Eli, his spiritual father, in order to better connect with his heavenly Father?

6. Younger and elder sons

What have you done? The voice of your brother's blood cries out to Me.

Genesis 4:10

There's room enough in God's heart for many sons and daughters. That's the good news.

Better than that, we don't have to compete to obtain our portion of the Father's love. His is a love that is multiplied when shared, not reduced to smaller portions as more brothers and sisters enter the family.

There is always enough. There always will be.

We don't need to kill our brother to get "our fair share of the cake".
We don't need to buy a birthright by inducing our brother to sell his.
We don't need to throw our brother (or sister) into a pit to obtain a coat-of-many-colours.
We don't need to exile Ishmael to have Isaac emerge as the son of promise.

There is room for everyone. God's heart is large enough. He's a good good father, Abba. He is also referred to as "the many-breasted-One" (El Shaddai—as in Psalm 91:1), which means that He can also provide a maternal kind of love.

And if ever blood needs to be shed to pay for something, an older brother already shed His to spare ours, a long time ago. No inversion needed in this family. The older brother pays the price, bites the dust, comes back with a coat-of-many-colours for each of us.

Isn't white indeed the combination of all other colours? And haven't we been promised white robes for the banqueting table?

Around this banqueting table, there is a seat reserved for every child. We don't need to play "musical chairs". Our name is written in the guest book, our place reserved; no "elbow-game" is needed. And a fattened calf has been provided to celebrate the presence of each one.

Younger and elder sons and daughters don't have to compete with one another, be jealous or greedy for what the other has received, monitor the inheritances. Everything will happen according to righteousness and truth. Nothing will be hidden, no need to expose or hide, no necessity to slander or backbite.

Positions around the table will be apportioned according to wise assessment. No need to strive to get to the top. There will be no pyramid or other triangular-power structure; it will be a banqueting table, probably round, as this is the best way to see and to get to know the many hosts.

We can't push ourselves into the place at the right or left hand of the Father. No need to.

But if we have spent all our (church) life attempting to gain such positions—would we be ready for this?

7. Fathers or pharaohs?

Let my people go!

Exodus 5:1 | 7:16 | 8:1 | 9:1…

You know that the rulers in this world lord it over their people, and officials flaunt their authority over those under them. But among you it will be different.

Matthew 20:25–26 NLT

Fathers try to build a family.
Pharaohs strive to erect a dynasty.

Fathers dream of joy for their children.
Pharaohs dream of success for their heirs.

Fathers spend time with their sons and daughters to share love with them.
Pharaohs entrust their heirs to others whose task is to transmit knowledge to them.

Fathers help sons find who they are and where their talents could best blossom. They want their sons to fulfil a calling.
Pharaohs secure heirs for their empires and fit them into their thrones. They want heirs to fill a position.

A father assembles a congregation.
A pharaoh builds an empire.

A father feeds a family.
A pharaoh feeds a structure.

A father provides for family members.
A pharaoh feeds on human resources.

A father extends a generous hand to his sons and daughters.
A pharaoh clutches one hand on the taxes and tithes of people and the other on his sceptre.

In both cases, something is being built.
With a father, living stones come together to form a family.
With a pharaoh, bricks are assembled to give shape to a pyramid.

Stones are precious, they deserve good care. If broken, time and energy needs to be invested to repair them and restore them to their beautiful and unique shape. If we can't add them to the building, something would be missing.

Bricks are a mere material, they have to fit. If needed, corners can be cut; standardisation of dimensions and shapes help save the time and energy of the builder. Useless bricks are thrown away and replaced by others which fit in better. One brick or another, who cares?

Sunday after Sunday, what are we erecting?
Which kingdom is being built?
A kingdom of freedom and love where the way we build is as important as the final construction?
A kingdom of enslavement and fear where the final result is what matters, no matter how and with whom the result is achieved?

Which structure is being prepared?
A banqueting table at which all may gather, feast together, grow and go?
A tower of Babel or pyramid for all to see, remember and make a

pedestal for the builder?

Who's making a name for whom in the building plans?
Who is it all about?
In which direction is the edifice pointing?

Honest answers to these questions would help us check what we are erecting and what kind of builders we are.
Let's think them through.

8. Sons and daughters coming of age

Rise up, my love, my fair one, and come away. For lo, the winter is past... the time of singing has come...

Song of Songs 2:10–12

In the lives of sons and daughters, there is one special moment when fathers are expected to be present—one very special event that they can hardly miss: the betrothal and marriage of their daughter, or son.

In certain cultures, preparations for this day begin long beforehand, pieces of clothing or furniture are collected, money set apart. When the daughter or son reaches young adulthood, the help of professional matchmakers is sometimes requested.

In the Bible, we see Eliezer being sent to another country to bring back a bride for Isaac. We see Esther being prepared for months before meeting the king and being made his queen. We see Ruth being helped by Naomi as well as Boaz to navigate the path out of widowhood and into a second and godly marriage.

In Jewish culture, a father would be preoccupied with the duty of arranging for the marriage of his son or daughter. It became a matter of concern if time passed and his daughter was still without any prospect of marriage. So much so that Laban tricked Jacob and gave him his older daughter Leah in place of the younger Rachel.

Horrible trick—yet borne out of a father's care towards his elder daughter and a desire to secure a posterity for her before she became too old to conceive.

The marriage of daughters was considered to be so much a father's responsibility that, in the New Testament, when Paul was addressing the question of staying single or marrying, he was not speaking to the children but directly to their fathers.

Fathers care about marrying their daughters and sons and about their posterity.

Is such care present in our churches today?

In European countries, statistics have been repeated for decades from the pulpits, often with nervous laughter: two thirds of the congregation (if not more) is made up of women; men are missing in the churches; for every eight young women of marriageable age present in the assembly, only two bachelors are available.

The problem is presented, statistics commented upon—and that's often all. If asked by one of the single ladies what action could be taken, pastors often answer: "Well, what can we do?"

Good question indeed, that spiritual fathers should take into consideration. At least, if no other idea comes to mind, the answer Jesus once gave to his disciples about a difficult situation they could not solve, could be: "*This kind can come out by nothing but prayer and fasting.*"[8]

New converts in countries saturated with dead religion, how can they come to Christ? By prayer and fasting.

Old bondages in the people filling the seats of our churches, how can they be broken? By prayer and fasting.

---

[8] Mark 9:29

Imbalance in our assemblies in numbers of men and women, how can it be readjusted? Prayer and fasting.

Indecisiveness of the few bachelors facing the many single ladies, how could it be solved? Prayer and fasting.

Discouragement in the waiting ladies (especially when entering their late thirties and the biological clock is beginning to tick), how could it be answered? Prayer and fasting.

You have not because you ask not.

Or you don't ask as you should. For social imbalances in our congregations, could it be that we should ask collectively?

Maybe spiritual fathers and mothers should go on their knees and ask: Why? What is the root cause of this issue? Is something blocking the way that should be removed?

As for many other situations of lack, someone is required to stand in the gap.
Someone who cares enough to lift the burden to the point of solution…

9. Where are the fathers?

My little children, for whom I labour in birth again until Christ is formed in you.

Galatians 4:19

When my father and my mother forsake me, then the Lord will take care of me.

Psalm 27:10

Lately, a lot has been said and written about a coming faceless generation. By this is meant that a people will arise to share the good news, without preoccupation of making a name or fame for themselves. That of course is a good point.

But a faceless generation, is this what we really want?

A crowd of people who can't be recognised, whose features can't be identified, whose identity remains uncertain? This would have the appearance of a fatherless generation, a generation not knowing who they are, where they come from nor where they are going. X-men and X-women of an X-generation that has been sacrificed by lack of investment in them.

According to sociology, such a generation exists. They are now in their late 40s or early 50s, the children of the "baby-boomers", born after the Second World War—this long period when men and fathers were missing. The X-generation in turn has given birth and place to the Y-generation—the millennials who grew up with a tablet or a smartphone in their hands and who were provided with television or video-games as their baby-sitters.

Y-generation people are said to take care first and foremost of themselves. In professional life, they could leave to travel the world, without giving much notice or consideration for the functioning of the team during their absence. They are "the children of divorce", the ones who grew up between houses and parents, the key of the door around their necks, with no one to take enough care of them.

Now they look after themselves.

This Y-generation has given way to the Z-generation or "digital natives"… Nobody is sure at this point how they will behave in their professional lives.

Where are the fathers?

From baby-boomers to baby-bombers, not much time has passed—just two or three generations. Nothing in terms of history. Yet time is accelerating.

Where are the fathers when sons decide to push the button that will make them explode into eternity, along with many others who had no choice about the matter?

Where are the fathers when the bombs are being prepared? When the belt is being fixed? When the last moment is approaching?

We hear about mothers having tried to intervene beforehand; mothers in tears after the very sad event, who participate in discussion groups with other mothers to share their pain and who try to avoid a repetition of such a thing ever happening again.

But where are the fathers?

Is somebody there, caring enough to stop, take time, listen and put an end to the faceless generation-process?

A cry to "Abba, Father" is rising from many orphan hearts in this hour.[9]

"Our Father who art in Heaven" is the way Jesus taught His disciples and followers to pray.

Father, our father—not a distant deity ruling over a spiritual empire, insisting on receiving tribute but too busy to really care about us.

Abba, Father. You, in whose image I have been created. You who care for me as the apple of Your eye.

Not Baal, my master, cold idol of wood who does not hear, see or feel, when I hurt...

---

[9] Those already secure in their identity do not need recognition to affirm it. But for the ones who had no "good enough fathers" or no father at all, the cry for adoption and affirmation is still there.

For leaders, it seems that it is hard to choose to father those children who do not look or act like them. They tend to only take on board those who make them feel good or, at least, do not represent too big a challenge. Yet adoption is a challenge, the challenge that a heavenly Father took and wants to encourage us to take, too.

The Answer

1. Let the wind blow and the prophet prophesy

On the day you were born your navel cord was not cut, nor were you washed in water to cleanse you; you were not rubbed with salt nor wrapped in swaddling cloths. No eye pitied you, to do any of these things for you, to have compassion on you; but you were thrown out into the open field, when you yourself were loathed on the day you were born. And when I passed by you and saw you struggling in your own blood, I said to you in your blood, "Live!"

Ezekiel 16: 4–6

Again He said to me, "Prophesy to these bones, and say to them, 'O dry bones, hear the word of the Lord!'"... So I prophesied as I was commanded; and as I prophesied, there was a noise, and suddenly a rattling; and the bones came together, bone to bone.

Ezekiel 37:4,7

"And I will pray the Father, and He will give you... the Spirit of truth... I will not leave you orphans; I will come to you."

John 14:16–18

In the beginning was the Word, and the Word was with God, and the Word was God.

In the beginning, God created the heavens and the earth. The earth was without form and void; and the Spirit of God was hovering over the chaos.

Word and spirit, from the beginning.

Word and spirit in the valley of dry bones to re-order the structure, bring bone back to bone and life back to the body.

"Live in your blood!"
"Come from the four winds, O breath, and breathe on those slain, that they may live!"

Prophesy, son of man, and let the dry bones hear the word of the Lord, again!
Speak and decree!

To all the young born-again babies—children and young adults who have been born and populate our churches, yet their cord has not been properly cut, too little water and salt have been applied and clothes are still missing—hear the word of your Father calling you to life, urging you, in your blood, to live!

Son of man, proclaim the good news again that the Father has sent His Son and His Spirit so that none should be left as an orphan!

As in Samuel's time, the Father is calling, piercing the night of silence and the deafness of ears.

Father, son, one another: His vocabulary speaks of family, adoption, inheritance, not of religious order, conforming to a system, pleasing a boss.

Will we return to the proclamation and release of this good news, this gospel of a God who took on flesh and blood and became Immanuel in order to be as close as possible to us? A God who loves us so much that He gave His only Son so that none should perish, but all would be gathered to Him in eternal life?

Speak and decree, son of man, tell the story again!

2. Let the scribe write

Then He said to them, "Therefore every scribe instructed concerning the kingdom of heaven is like a householder who brings out of his treasure things new and old."

Matthew 13:52

My tongue is the pen of a ready writer.

Psalm 45: 1

Write the vision and make it plain on tablets, that he may run who reads it.

Habakkuk 2:2

It's a very old story, a very old treasure, this love letter of God to man, of a Father to his sons. Yet centuries of history and church practices have deposited a film of sand upon the words. Some hearts, ears, eyes, have turned cold or are completely closed.

It's time for new pens to write, time for modern scribes to tell the old story in a new way. Engrave it on tablets, tablets of the heart, so that the stone can become flesh again. Write the vision and make it plain for all to see.

How to write when everything has been said and written, yet the words have not been heard, and names have been ill-used? When

God the Father has been turned into The Godfather, a character we would prefer not to meet?

A similar challenge was faced centuries ago, when a young Augustinian monk found himself copying the Bible and reading it, rediscovering a story of grace, simplicity and love that had little in common with the one told by the Roman church of his time.

What could be done?

Did he hear the same voice and words as the prophet Habakkuk of old? History does not tell us. Yet we find Martin Luther (the young monk we are speaking about), on a spring day in 1517, five centuries ago, nailing on the door of the local church, plain for all to see, his 95 theses aimed at restoring the church closer to its original blueprint. Telling the story once again, translating it into a language people could understand, having it printed, distributed and discussed throughout Europe.

His was certainly the pen of a ready writer, when it came to bringing the Bible close to the people again.

Martin Luther was a scribe during a time of reformation.

In such a season, writing tends to increase.

Let the words be released and not held back, as the Spirit is hovering once again, whispering words, old and new, in the ears of little Samuels and old Habakkuks.

3. Let saviours arise

"But on Mount Zion there shall be deliverance and there shall be holiness...
Then saviours shall come to mount Zion to judge the mountains of Esau. And the kingdom shall be the Lord's."

Obadiah 1:17, 21

"This is the word of the Lord to Zerubbabel: Not by might nor by power but by My Spirit, says the Lord of hosts... And he shall bring forth the capstone with shouts of 'Grace, grace to it!'"

Zechariah 4:6–7

The Bible is very clear about the fact that one Saviour and Messiah is enough to reconnect us to the Father, and that Jesus is this perfect saviour; that by His death and resurrection He gained the right to send us a Helper, the Spirit of Truth, so that we would not be left as orphans.

Yet, although Jesus paid the full price and Holy Spirit has been released, along with the spirit of adoption and sonship, many in our churches today still feel like orphans.

How does this happen? What else can be done about it?

In the book of Obadiah, the smallest book of the Bible, we see something quite interesting. We read that: *"Then saviours shall come to mount Zion."* The word used there is *moshiim*, "deliverers". Obadiah here is not prophesying about the coming Messiah, singular, but about the coming of a multiplicity of deliverers, in the plural.

An etymological study shows that it is referring to judges. Hebrew judges were saviours for the people in the sense that they liberated them from the oppression of foreigners, provided help for widows and orphans and executed justice in disputes among men. Such a judge was Deborah who was also a prophetess. She sat under a palm tree whilst judging Israel. Interestingly enough, she is also referred to as "a mother in Israel".[10]

Saviours shall come—deliverers, judges, mothers. Fathers also, perhaps?

Could it be that, in order for the church to manifest perfect deliverance and salvation and embody perfect adoption, more fathers need to arise?

Could it be that we still need more people in our churches to speak up as Paul the apostle did to the many who still feel like orphans:

My dear children, for whom I am again in the pains of childbirth until Christ is formed in you.[11]

For though you have countless guides in Christ, you do not have many fathers.[12]

Such a one I aspire to be to you... [13]

And how would fathers be able to rise up, able to father others whilst they themselves often lacked spiritual parents in their own lives?

---

[10] Judges 4:4–5 and 5:7
[11] Galatians 4:19
[12] 1 Corinthians 4:15 ESV
[13] Addition from the writer

How would a generation X be able to father a generation Y or Z whilst identities have not been affirmed enough by past generations?

How do we pass on to sons what we have not received from our fathers?

This is a whole book in itself, but we begin by inviting the capstone back, Jesus, into the structure, pleading for grace, grace!

He is our older brother, He knows the way to the Father.

He is also the Chief Cornerstone and knows how to build His church.

4. Prodigals coming home

Behold, I will send you Elijah the prophet, before the coming of the great and dreadful day of the Lord. And he will turn the hearts of the fathers to the children, and the hearts of the children to the fathers, lest I come and strike the earth with a curse.

Malachi 4:5–6

It's time for the prodigals to come home. And the prodigals are many—as we can read in Hemingway's story, *Capital of the World*. In it, the writer tells the tale of a Spanish father who is searching for his son Paco. The boy has run away from home after a fight between the two of them. The father so badly wants a reconciliation with his son that, when he realises the chances of finding him by walking the streets are very slim, he places an advertisement in the local newspaper. "Paco, meet me at the Hotel Montana at noon on Tuesday. All is forgiven! Love, Papa."

The following Tuesday at noon, eight hundred young men named Paco were waiting outside the hotel Montana to receive the father's embrace of forgiveness…

Today too, in real life, many Paco's and Paquita's are waiting for an invitation to reconcile in numerous "Hotels Montana" all over the world.

It's time for prodigals to come home. And it's time for fathers to open their arms wide and welcome them warmly.

Too long have they been deprived of each other. Too long have they been separated on diverging or parallel roads that could only cross at infinity.

Well, there we are. Infinity.

Infinity of love is indeed needed.

Hearts of the fathers being drawn again to children, hearts of children being drawn again to fathers. A wind needs to blow, warm and strong, to bridge the gap and gather fathers and children together as they desperately need one another.

Prodigals having left churches as they experienced much of structure and expectations and little of family and acceptance. Prodigals who sometimes had a sharper eye than their older brothers, who stayed there for decades, not really enjoying the stay (no reason to feast, no fatted calf to prepare due to lack of reasons to celebrate) but out of a (false?) sense of duty.

Like the wild men in David's time, prodigals left for the desert, the caves of Adullam,[14] where they shared company with other wild men who could not fit into the system—yet were in search of a community and a leader.

A man after God's heart, David must have had an ability to father—his nation, if not his own family. Not duplicate the religious system, but transmit a hunger for God and a thirst to answer His call and become the men (and women) that He had called them to be.

Fight for righteousness and justice, for a kingdom that had yet to be built and a land that still had to be conquered.

Prodigals of all kinds, having left for good or bad reasons, need to come back home. The road has been long and dusty, with much

---
[14] 1 Samuel 22:1–2

wounding. Things have been lost, other things maybe added, during this exodus in far-away countries. Yet the love of the father is still missing and calling.

Things have to be turned around in the fathers' heart. Forgiveness needs to penetrate more deeply. Healing needs to take place. Areas have to be touched in the sons' and daughters' hearts. A coming to oneself, an assessment of the road, a softening or breaking of the heart. Movement has to resume in both of them.

Fathers need to prepare, get out, go onto the road, watch and see what and who is coming.

Sons need to set their feet on the path.

Older sons need to check their hearts.

Fattened calves have to be brought and mothers need to prepare tables.[15]

A wind, strong and warm, is beginning to blow, pushing sons and fathers in their backs, urging them to reassemble. Churches have to prepare. Seating will soon be insufficient; space will need to be enlarged—in hearts at first.

Enlarge the space of your tent, stretch your tent curtains wide, do not hold back; lengthen your cords, strengthen your stakes. For you will spread out to the right and to the left.[16]

Enlarge, church, indeed, don't hold back.

More is in you.

More sons and daughters need to come in.

---

[15] No mention of a mother in the biblical story. Maybe this father was a widow? But it is with a purpose that we here make mention of mothers as, in the coming restoration/ reformation, they will also have an important role to play.

[16] Isaiah 54:2–3

Afterword: About the coming Wind

THE WIND BLOWS where it wants.

The Wind of God blows where He wants, and this wind is about to blow again across the world, not as a sweet little breeze but as a tempestuous whirlwind aimed at bringing back the order and structure from Above, the bone structure of God back to the Body of Christ.

Let he and she who has an ear hear—the first tremblings are already in the air.

The Spirit moves upon the surface of the bones, and so backbones are being restored in order to be able to carry the revival that everybody is speaking about—without knowing too well how to hasten its coming.

Structures, a structural divine order, is being restored, which will serve the divine purposes. Amongst those structures are the family; the relationships between men and women, parents and children.

Hear the Wind and the noise of bones coming back into place: He comes!

And when this Wind comes, don't resist Him: position yourself in such a way that He would blow in your back and take you where He desires.

Let yourself be connected or reconnected to those bones—don't resist Him in the name of a well-meaning but wrongly understood faithfulness to your old bone structure.

See, God is doing a new thing. Would you not perceive it?

God comes, not in a superficial way but in the very structure of our being, not in the packaging of our churches but in the very structure of His Body—bone of His bone, flesh of His flesh. God comes and He has His own idea about the structure He needs for His purposes.

Will we align ourselves with His plans and follow Him in His ways—or will we go on imposing on Him our own structures, good ideas and programs?

Will we follow the move that He initiates and let ourselves be carried along by His wave—or will we resist Him and wrestle with Him, using all our strength to maintain old, dry and dying structures in place?

"Behold, I have put My words in your mouth. See, I have this day set you over the nations and over the kingdoms. To root out and to pull down, to destroy and to throw down, to build and to plant."

Jeremiah 1:9–10

None of us knows where He comes from nor where He is going. But we can perceive the movement and decide to let Him carry us.

By the way, this is the only reasonable thing to do when bones begin to fly about with the force of a whirlwind: obey the wind so that you will not be crushed. When bones begin to join up with other bones in accordance with divine order, a mighty army will arise, ready for battle. At the same time, real family will be birthed: bone of my bone, flesh of my flesh, spirit of my spirit—finally, I am joined to another to give birth, according to my species, according to the order from Above. Real unity is created, covenants of one flesh, threefold cords that won't be easily broken. Unions of heart, spirit, vision which will finally make it possible to take possession of the promised land.

Come, Lord, come, and blow from the four winds!

Acknowledgements

To my earthly father, Charles Dekker, for having been such a good loving father to me, having prepared my heart for the love of a Heavenly Father.

To my Father in Heaven, for having adopted the orphan I had become and for making this adoption more real every day.

To the ones I recognise as spiritual fathers and mothers in my land and also, in some or many aspects, in my life: Anne, "a mother in Israel, Belgium, and many other lands", Rick and Sabine, Jan and Debbie, Luc and Agnès, Ignace and Miet, Yves and Liliane…

To the ones who have helped with this book: Moyra and Graham, Elisabeth, Pierre, Eric, Wytze…

To all those—pastors or others—who, during all those years as a Christian in Belgium or abroad, have been overseeing my life, doing the best they could.

Being a father or a son/daughter is not easy. We all have to keep learning.

www.ingramcontent.com/pod-product-compliance
Lightning Source LLC
Chambersburg PA
CBHW021123080526
44587CB00010B/622